SEX AIN'T THE WAY TO LOVE

© 2025 Tavia Mapp-Deterville

All rights reserved. No part of this book may be copied, stored, or shared in any form without written permission from the publisher, except in the case of brief quotations used in reviews or scholarly work.

Published by: Cultureel Stories

www.cultureelstories.com

This book is a work of nonfiction and represents the personal experiences, insights, and perspectives of the author. While every effort has been made to ensure accuracy, the publisher and author assume no responsibility for any errors or omissions.

ISBN: 979-8-9993654-0-8

First Edition

Contents

Chapter One - It's Not Them, It's You.. 1

Chapter Two - All the Ships (Friendship, Situationship, Relationship)....10

Chapter Three - You're The One... 20

Chapter Four - Sometimes I Touch Myself 28

Chapter Five - It Had To Be You.. 35

Chapter Six - I Was Lost But Now I'm Found... 45

Dedication.. 52

Chapter One

It's Not Them, It's You

G reetings to you and yours. Lean in close as I dispel to you the words that your friends couldn't get through to you, that your parents can't fix for you, and that your kids can't help you with. I need you to know right now before we get any further in this conversation that your pussy ain't shit.

Let me continue by saying, I am not a doctor. I have not received a degree in psychology. I have not minored in behavioral studies and everything you are about to read is based solely on experience, observation, and listening for hours to complaining friends. Not only that but being that complaining friend. I may not have whined about it the way they have though. Now that I think of it, I should have been paid for it! At least when they opted to ignore the advice they begged for, I didn't feel offended. Like most of us, we have all been in a failed relationship. We have read books and watched movies like. "Think Like A Man". We have watched Netflix shows like "Love is Blind" wishing we had a man like Cameron and listened intently to see if we can follow the blueprint of finding your person. What I need you to do is stop. If you are a man or woman reading this, you will not find love until you first do the work of literally figuring out what you want, unloading your hurt and being selfish enough to love yourself most. Nothing is perfect. I mean you could order fries from McDonald's. They are fresh, hot, salted but there are still going to be a couple that are soggy. A couple that are burnt but you keep eating them, right? You don't throw them away. You push through what you thought and enjoy what you got. Now while some may see that as settling, it's not. It's realizing that you have what you want. Simple. Now girls may run the world, but good sex keeps it spinning. It's because of good sex that women and men allow messed up people to continue to stick around. Call it stupidity, low self-esteem or just plain not wanting to be alone, but the moment you compromise what you know in your core to be right, you my dear are fucked. Royally flushed. Whatever happens next will become the things you will spend days, months, even years attempting to get over.

    Not everything can be solved via therapy. Not everything you can continue to bury and pretend it doesn't exist. You gotta do the work. Dance the dance. You have to look in the mirror and ask if you are happy with yourself. Until you can say yes, no one can make it yes for you. Now this may be a bit all over the place, but you catch my drift. You get that you must figure out what is about you that attracts ain't shit people. It can't be everyone else all the time. We live in this place where taking ownership of your own stuff is only okay when you are pointing the finger at someone else. Everyone wants to play the victim. Everyone wants to stand up and say they messed up. No one wants to stand with a smoking gun, staring into your eyes and confess they shot the sheriff, but they didn't shoot the deputy. They want to say he made me do it. He pushed me. He provoked me. He forced my hand. None of this changes that you shot him, so actually none of those words matter. Instead of looking for an out, start by being honest.

Start by being hopeful. Start by being yourself and if you don't know who that is, stop and spend some time with yourself. Every love story is a stream of self-discovery. The whole story doesn't have to fit but there will be jewels that you find if you open your mind and heart to it. Understand that in order to get what you want; you may have to live through some scary shit. You think it's easy to love, easy to accept yourself let alone someone else. You think it's easy to be vulnerable to tell someone exactly how you feel and not think the whole time what they are thinking. Well it's not. If it was you wouldn't be single or sitting with someone you secretly can't stand.

Before you start to wonder who the hell do I think I am to call you out like this, I know because all of this was me. I thought because I was slim, weave tight, smile that lit up a room, gave a bomb ass blow job with a tight pussy, I was the shit. I was the Boss. I was in charge and when I snapped my fingers any man would be at my feet. If they couldn't do what I wanted, then they would be dismissed. I had no idea what it meant to work it out. Had no idea what it meant to even act like a lady because I was too busy making every man know that I didn't need them. It wasn't even their fault. I had been around men my whole life that figured if they did what they were supposed to in the bedroom, they could get any woman to do what they wanted and believe everything they said. No matter how crazy it was. Let me tell you, that wasn't gonna be me. I wasn't about to get caught up in the matrix. I wasn't about to look like nobody's fool because that is exactly what I felt these women were. It wasn't until I got older that I realized how much you will compromise just to feel loved. How much you would sacrifice just to feel needed. But when you find someone that looks like they may actually be able to reciprocate the love you want to give now that is when the fun starts. Just as inviting and uplifting as the intro to Amerie's Why Don't We Fall in Love creeps from your speakers, you are instantly connected. Aware of their every move, excited by their every word and lustful to every crevice of their body. It's amazing. It's freeing. It's everything the books and the movies and the songs said it would be until it's not. Then the calls are replaced with texts and the texts come in far and few between. Then you find yourself online scanning for clues as to why all of a sudden, they have disappeared. You try to distract yourself with your friends but since you faded to black, you are no longer a part of the hangouts and brunch dates. It is automatically assumed you are busy and instantly you feel left out. You wonder what happened to your identity. You feel stupid for all the times you traded the I's for We's and hear your mama in the back of your mind saying why buy the cow when you can get the milk for free? Was it too early? Were you the only one falling and you didn't realize it until you got that dreadful awkward call from them with a bunch of meaningless excuses about why they were absent. How they needed to take a break. The words drift in the air as you literally wonder what really happened. What will you say about why you are no longer posting them every week on crush days or why you are no longer tagging them in every single status update and why now you are so damn available. I mean if it's not them, is it you? Then you remember they are on the phone and you quickly make up a reason to get off to save face. I mean this call was for their closure not yours. So fuck em. On to the next, I mean literally.

Before we go further, I need you to understand something: **change begins with you.** You may not realize it, but your experiences, actions, and choices shape the people and situations you attract. Let's dive into why that's true and what you can do to break unhealthy patterns and embrace self-love.

Reflection: The Tough Questions

1. **Self-Assessment**: What are the patterns in your relationships? Are there similarities in the kinds of people you attract or the dynamics that unfold?
   Write about your most recent or significant relationships. What worked? What didn't?

2. **Responsibility Check**: Have you ever blamed others for situations that didn't go your way? How much of that blame belongs to you?
   List one instance where you might have shifted responsibility. How could you have approached it differently?

Exercise: Mirror Work

1. Stand in front of a mirror. Look yourself in the eyes and ask: **Am I happy with myself?**
   - If the answer is yes, write down why.
   - If the answer is no, write what you believe is missing.

2. Repeat this affirmation:
   "I am learning to love myself fully. I will take responsibility for my growth and happiness."

   How does it feel to say this? Write about your emotions and thoughts.

Action: Identifying Your Core Desires

You cannot find the right relationship until you know what you want and need.

- **What do you value most in a partner?** (e.g., honesty, stability, humor)
- **What boundaries are non-negotiable for you?**
- **What do you need to work on within yourself to attract someone who respects and complements you?**

Journal Prompt: Unloading Your Hurt

Write about a past experience where you felt heartbroken, rejected, or betrayed. Answer the following:

1. How did you process those feelings at the time?
2. What would you say to your younger self about that situation now?
3. How can you let go of the lingering pain?

Visualization: Your Ideal Future

Close your eyes and imagine the best version of yourself in a healthy, loving relationship.

- What does your day-to-day life look like?
- How do you feel about yourself?
- How do you and your partner support and uplift each other?

Open your journal and write this vision in detail

Note to Self

More to Say..

Chapter Two

○ ◇ ○

All the Ships (Friendship, Situationship, Relationship)

Now let's say none of that happened and you met someone and said let's get to know each other. Let's be friends. In most cases you just shot yourself in the foot because if you are a friend, you will never be anything more and it will take an act of Jesus before you are seen as anything else. This does not mean they won't kiss you or have sex with you or compare everyone they are actually seeing to you. It will mean that you will be an option. Remember options don't always get picked. They get paraded around to ensure whomever they want is aware there is another contender. I mean who doesn't want someone that someone else wants or has. It's the thrill of the chase. You ever notice how someone becomes five times more attractive when they are with someone else. I mean it's even how we shop. We see someone wearing something and in our minds, we could have worn it better so we give a dry compliment with the sole intention of letting that person know that we see you. So again, never say you want to be friends unless you only want to be friends and that's it. On the flipside, what if you meet someone and there is instant chemistry. You have been hanging out. You have gone on a couple dates, felt each other up, sent silly emoji and you look forward to hearing from them. Things can go in one of two directions after sex because guess what it's coming up next. It is true that a woman knows instantly if she is gonna sleep with someone. Your job is not to fuck it up and if you're smart you know that so divulging that you aren't ready for a relationship never happens before the clothes come off. Mentioning, you may be seeing someone else also never comes up. No matter what the intentions, pussy doesn't have a face. Someone is warmer, they react differently and have better rhythm but eventually you will have to deal with the person it's attached to. Hence is how situationships are born. Now if the last few sentences went in another direction and a dude fell into you and said this the place for me then by golly you are in a relationship. Hook line and sinker. That man will confess his undying affection for you and have no issue claiming you politically and socially and quickly accept your invitation to be together on Facebook, whether he uses it or not. Different rules for different relationships. But situationships my people are what every Jerry Springer, Divorce Court, and Dr. Phil show is made of.

    There is nothing more confusing than allowing someone to float in and out of your life leaving trails of condoms and random late night calls behind them. Now we are all grown and for some of this is exactly all we want. I went through a whole summer of thottin in these streets. Fucking faces and not returning calls. Coming and going if you catch that alley oop. I remember working at a retail store and eyeing this younger guy that would come in with his mother. I cared nothing about him being 6 years younger than me, I was 26 by the way. All I saw was his beautiful eyes, muscles and tattoos. I have no problem letting the judgment in your mind run a marathon because I wasn't trying to marry him. That had situationship written all over it. Randomly meeting his older brother and dating him was just a mess. I know what it's like to not know what you want nor the desire to figure it out. I also know what it's like to wake up in the middle of the night to your own sobs because the emptiness that not choosing brings. Then denial allows you to brush it off and live to thot another day. To lose yourself in the dance of living in the moment until reality kicks you in the ass and any random scenario wakes you up from the bliss you ignorantly participated in. Like you get pregnant, or you bump into their other mate or you get chlamydia or after fucking for hours you realize they are all you want and you trap them into a decision and it's not you. No matter what happens the first thing that will come to your mind is SHIT! Is this really happening?? And just as quickly, your mind responds yes, it is. Now it's time to deal with it. This is when it gets real and if you're smart you make a decision based on what is best for you. Like your mind and heart not your love below. Now, if your heart and mind don't agree, you will feel like you're totally screwed. This is one of those moments that you take a step back and literally attempt to get to know yourself. The closer you get to knowing who you are the easier any future decision will become easy like Sunday morning. Now make sure you take this time to do it. This is a teachable moment people and no matter what comes on the other side you should be wiser. You should be a bit stronger. But if you don't do the work. If you don't take the time and you continue to thrust yourself deeper and deeper within this web you've weaved no good will come of it. You will become bitter. You will become one of those men or women standing on their Facebook soapbox complaining about how the mate they chose wasn't worth nothing. Don't do it. Back away from the twitter beef and grow the hell up. It will only make you appear bitter and trust me no one wants to be lonely and bitter. All of this still leads back to you. Until you know what you want and not entertain anything else other than that then drama will follow. I mean even Ciara belted out sadly, "right now what's killing me cause now I have to find someone else when all I wanted was you" to Future before the prayer that led to her becoming Mrs. Wilson.

Reflection: Defining the "Ships" in Your Life

1. **Friendship**:
    - Have you ever started a friendship hoping it would evolve into something more? What happened?
    - Write about a current or past friendship where the boundaries became blurred. How did it affect you?

2. **Situationship**:
    - Have you ever been in a situationship? How did it start, and what was your emotional state during it?
    - Were there moments where you ignored red flags or settled for less than you deserved?

3. **Relationship**:
    - Think about your most recent relationship. What worked? What didn't?
    - Did you compromise too much or not enough?

Activity: Relationship Patterns

On a sheet of paper or in your journal, create three columns labeled:

- **Friendships**
- **Situationships**
- **Relationships**

Under each column, write down examples from your life. Reflect on these questions:

- What patterns or similarities do you notice?
- How have these experiences shaped your views on love and connection?

Exercise: Setting Boundaries

Boundaries are essential for healthy relationships. Without them, you risk becoming an option rather than a priority.

1. Write down three non-negotiable boundaries for:
    - Friendships
    - Situationships
    - Relationships
2. For each boundary, explain why it's important and how you will uphold it.

Journal Prompt: Your Ideal Partner

Imagine your ideal partner. Describe them in detail, focusing on qualities that go beyond physical appearance, such as:

- Communication style
- Emotional intelligence
- Shared values

Then ask yourself:

- Are these qualities reflected in the people I currently entertain?
- If not, what can I do to align my actions with my desires?

Visualization: Living Without Drama

Close your eyes and visualize a drama-free version of your life. What does it look like?

- How do you handle relationships?
- What kind of people surround you?
- How do you feel about yourself?

Write about this vision and steps you can take to make it your reality.

Action: Navigating Tough Decisions

Sometimes, you must choose between your heart, mind, and "love below." When faced with tough decisions, try this:

1. **Pause**: Take a step back and assess the situation.
2. **Evaluate**: Ask yourself: "What do I want? What do I need?"
3. **Decide**: Make a choice based on what aligns with your values, not just fleeting feelings.

Write about a time when you had to make a tough relationship decision. How did you handle it? What did you learn?

Affirmation: Growing Stronger

Repeat this affirmation to yourself:

"I deserve relationships that align with my values and respect my boundaries. I will choose connection over convenience and love over loneliness."

Note to Self

More to Say..

Chapter Three

You're The One

I've probably told this story a couple times before and it literally became a request so why not share it with you. I mean we are friends now. You have been reading this so far so why not. I had been dating this guy let's call him Adam and after months of bomb sex, meeting his family and talks of marriage and children, I found out via a DM on Facebook that he was married. She got the courage to do it because she found out she was pregnant and figured if I knew I would leave him alone. Well of course I would but that didn't stop the pain I felt. What made it worse is I found out that he had been telling people I was stalking him. Now I'm not a ten but I'm a strong 8 and stalking any man was far beneath me. I aired him out and exposed him to everyone that would listen. No one believed me until he began to lie to them. It's funny how women are often the bad guy until the guy proves to be a piece of shit. When the dust settled, the pain really set in. I gave myself my normal forty-eight hours to cry and feel bad for myself before I shook it off and started to pick myself up. Except this time, I could not shake the hurt. Two days turned into ten and I just couldn't understand why I couldn't find someone for me. I began to binge watch comedy movies literally looking for my smile. Looking for any reminisce of me.

I had this bootleg copy of like three of Kat Williams's stand-ups. The first and second seemed to play and I found a chuckle here and there but no smile. I sat up in my bed convinced I need to remind myself who I was. I mean I had gone on for years acting like a man. Literally, only needing someone to keep my bed warm and disguising it as a relationship. It had been years since I felt this hurt. My trance was broken by Katt's voice. "Ladies! On the other hand, if you are twenty-five years old and you are still walking around saying men ain't shit, you need to get a handle on your motherfuckin life and take responsibility chick! What you mean to say all the men you fuck with ain't shit. You need to figure out what's wrong with your pussy that keeps attracting ain't shit men." Now of course he didn't say men or chick but you don't need that vulgarity to catch what became my epiphany. I was 31 years old. I laid back thinking of the last three relationships that I had been in. Their images came to mind. Everything about them was so similar, they could have been cousins. So right there, you have a type. That type ain't working for you. So right then, I stood up in my bed and I broke up with every man that I would meet that look, talk or act like the men of my past. I grabbed a book and wrote down what I needed in a man. At first the requests were simple, someone taller than me, job, and could lay it down in the bedroom. I decided to be abstinent until I found it. Now I'm not saying that is what you should do. It wasn't easy, like at all. The more I started to be ok with it, the more men started to literally throw out offers to do whatever I wanted to allow them to break my vow. I couldn't. I had to figure out what I wanted. More importantly, what I needed.

One day, I had a dream and I could see me as a child crying. Listening to my mother tell my stepfather that she didn't need him as the smoke left her cigarette. I could see his face becoming angry and hurt as she told him that if he didn't like it, he could leave. When she said those words, the dream warped to different moments when I said those exact words. I woke up in a cold sweat with tears still coming from my eyes. It was a sign. There were wounds I needed to heal. I couldn't go on with my life pretending I needed no one. I had to learn to let people in. I had to learn to let myself in. I mean how could I expect anyone to love me when I didn't even know who I was. I felt like the part in Runaway Bride when Richard Gere outs Julia Roberts for not even knowing how she liked her eggs. I took so much pride in taking care of everyone and being there for anyone that I failed to realize that I sucked at loving myself. It was true and that was ok. I mean at least I knew what was wrong. You know how long it takes someone people to realize what is really wrong with them. Some sacrifice thousands of dollars and hours in therapy. Some don't figure it out at all. The key thing was how to fix it. Despite watching countless episodes of Being Mary Jane and being inspired by the post it notes, I had no desire to spew affirmations to myself every morning. The realist side of me would just laugh. So I did what I knew would lift my spirits. I made two playlists. The songs that would affect my spirit and others that would make my ass pop and remind me of my swag. Before I knew it, I was getting out of the shower, trying to keep up with Coko as she belted out, You're the one, and it hit me. I was happy. I was not just content but happy. The smile on my face wasn't forced, wasn't planned and masked nothing. It was my mood and I was grateful. I dried my skin, lotion my body and got dressed. Off into the world I went. Happy to be seen. I felt rescued. I felt whole. Now if only I could lose these pesky pounds life would be perfect.

Reading Break Activity (I mean why not)

Relationships often act as mirrors, reflecting back what we need to heal or change. From what I shared previously; the heartbreak of betrayal led to an epiphany: the realization that recurring patterns often have deeper roots. Whether it's the type of partner you attract or the ways you protect yourself from vulnerability, recognizing these patterns is the first step toward change.

Take some time to reflect deeply on these questions. Write your answers in your journal, or better yet, create a dedicated space where you can return to these thoughts and continue to build self-awareness.

1. **What is something you always love doing, even when you are tired or rushed?**
    - Write about how this activity brings you joy or energy. How can you incorporate more of it into your daily life?
2. **What do you believe is possible for you?**
    - Consider your dreams and goals. Are you holding yourself back in any way?
3. **What does real love look like for you?**
    - Describe in detail what a loving, supportive relationship feels like. How does it align with your current or past relationships?

4. **What are your deal breakers?**

- List five non-negotiable values or behaviors that you will not compromise on in relationships. Why are these important to you?

5. **What about yourself might be deal breakers for someone else?**
    - Be honest and compassionate. Are there behaviors or traits you could improve?

6. **What are you willing to sacrifice?**
    - In pursuit of a meaningful relationship, what are you willing to let go of, and what remains non-negotiable?

7. **How comfortable are you with being alone?**
    - Write about how you feel when you're by yourself. Do you enjoy your own company? If not, what steps can you take to improve this relationship with yourself?

8. **Do you hold grudges?**
    - Reflect on unresolved issues. How might forgiveness (for yourself or others) free you from lingering negativity?

9. **How do you let someone know what you are thinking and feeling?**
    - Think about your communication style. Are you open and direct, or do you hold back? How does this affect your relationships?

10. **What is most important to you?**
    - Write a list of your core values. How do these values guide your decisions in life and love?

Exercise: Your Self-Love Playlist

Music can be a powerful tool for transformation. Create two playlists like the I did:

1. **Spirit Playlist**: Fill this with songs that uplift and inspire you, reminding you of your strength and resilience.
2. **Swag Playlist**: Add songs that make you feel confident, sexy, and unstoppable.

Whenever you feel down or unsure of yourself, turn to these playlists to reconnect with your power.

Activity: Breaking the Cycle

Think about your relationship patterns. Answer the following questions in your journal:

- What similarities do you notice between your past partners?
- What qualities in them attracted you, and why didn't it work out?
- What lessons did you learn from these experiences?

Now, write a "break-up letter" to the type of person you're no longer willing to entertain. Be specific and clear about what you're letting go of and why.

Affirmation: Embracing Self-Worth

Repeat this affirmation to yourself daily:

> "I am whole, worthy, and deserving of love. I will attract relationships that align with my highest self."

Note to Self

More to Say..

Chapter Four

◇ ◇ ◇

Sometimes I Touch Myself

For a long time, my thoughts went back and forth through the lyrics of MJB's "My Life" and "Be Happy". Then I realized I had no idea what it meant to be happy. I didn't know how I felt. I didn't know what I liked. I didn't even know if I liked me. I mean I was literally living for my daughter. I was keeping up appearances and smiling for the camera but when I walked out the door and into the back of my cab, I would cry all the way home. I was popular, I commanded everyone's attention and I had a ton of friends but I was lonely. To add insult to injury, I didn't know if I was lonely or felt alone. You know movies are really the stories of my life. I am the biggest Julia Roberts fan and I remember watching Runaway Bride and Richard Gere spewing at Julia that she didn't even know how she liked her eggs. Immediately, I cringed. I mean it was literally at that moment I began to wonder what I liked. I mean as a woman we sit and we say of these generic things we want from our mate. I admit it was me as well. I wanted a man that was tall, attractive, had a job, liked kids, romantic and had a remote control between his legs. So, I looked for that. I found that but I realized it wasn't all I wanted. I've come to realize that some people who have those qualities are cheaters. Some are emotionally unavailable. Some also have no idea what they want. Some get to the finish line before you. Some are even more hurt than you are. That is when I realized you got to be more specific about what you actually want. The kicker was realizing I didn't know what that was.

I started reading relationship magazines and books. I was watching Dr. Phil and Oprah Master Class but I was exhausted. Exhausted from wondering when I would be in this amazing relationship. Exhausted from everyone asking me when I would be married and have more children. Exhausted from carrying the weight of everyone's opinions. Until I said fuck it. If I'm gonna be alone, I'm gonna be happy. Happy because I am here. Happy because my daughter loves me. Happy Because I make good money and can go wherever I want. Happy because I can still fit those jeans I think fits me so well. I'm just gonna smile. I'm gonna stop turning down invites to hang out then regretting it later. I'm gonna spend time with the people that truly care about me, reinforcing the importance of caring about myself. It was at that moment I started to care more about myself. I started researching myself, taking notice of the moments I laughed the hardest. My head was clear. My heart was open, and I even started sleeping better. Then one night something weird happened. I had this weird dream. I was talking to my dad, and I was telling him how much his absence hurt me. The dream felt so real that I woke up with tears running down my face. I grabbed my notebook from the side of my bed and I wrote at the top, "My Perfect Mate". Under it, I wrote, someone that I won't worry about leaving me. Someone that loves me more than I love them. Now before you curse me out my grandmother always told me that you should be with someone that loves you just a little bit more than you love them. It keeps them feeling grateful to have you. If you love them more than chances, are he is gonna leave you for someone else. So, it stayed with me. Then I wrote to someone who understands when I need my space. Someone that is trusting and loving. Someone that matches my sex drive. Someone that supports my dreams. Someone who makes me laugh and is truly my best friend. I closed the book and went back to sleep. It was as though I gave it to God. I didn't pray like Ciara but I did hand it over to him. I guess the part that felt the best was that I felt like it was for me. What I wanted was exactly what fit my heart. I mean some of the things on my list could have been what other women wanted but not everything. I think when you make a list like that he should feel far from generic. It should feel like your diamond in the rough. It should feel right in your spirit. Once you have released into the atmosphere what you want, you gotta stay open to receive it and keep being positive. Now for all those nasty people waiting for the moment where I let on about touching myself literally, that never happened. I don't know how to masturbate. I mean I love myself but I guess that to that extent. What I touched was my heart. Keep it clean people. Keep it clean.

Enhanced Reading Break Activity

Take a moment to dive deeper into your thoughts and feelings. Reflect on these questions in your journal or as a guided meditation.

1. **When was the last time you felt genuinely happy?**
   - What were you doing, and who were you with? How can you create more moments like this?

2. **What do you enjoy doing that is entirely for you?**
   - Consider hobbies, passions, or small moments of joy that you don't share with anyone else.

3. **How do you define happiness for yourself?**
   - Write a few sentences about what happiness feels like to you—not what it looks like to others.

4. **What external pressures or expectations are you ready to let go of?**
   - Reflect on societal or personal expectations that no longer serve you.

5. **What makes you feel loved?**
   - List five things, big or small, that make you feel appreciated and cared for.

6. **What is one thing you've always wanted to do but haven't?**
   - Plan one small step toward making this dream a reality.

Exercise: Creating Your Perfect Mate List

Take inspiration from my story and create your own list of qualities for a perfect mate. Go beyond the surface—dig deep into what aligns with your heart and values.

Instructions:

- Include traits that reflect emotional, intellectual, and physical compatibility.
- Be specific but stay true to what genuinely matters to you.

Affirmation: Letting Go and Staying Open

Repeat this affirmation daily:

> "I am worthy of love, joy, and peace. I trust the universe to guide me toward what is meant for me."

Note to Self

More to Say..

Chapter Five

It Had To Be You

I guess when you find the love of self you find the love of others. Well I think that's how it should go. I was on the bus going to get my nails done on a brisk afternoon because my birthday was coming. I had travelled all the way to Long Island to get my hair colored and styled so I was feeling amazing. I started playing on my phone and came across my bible app and decided to read. As soon as it opened the Daily Scripture read, "He who finds a wife, finds a good thing". I instantly stared at the words and wondered what that meant exactly. I mean was this like a game of hide and seek and I was supposed to wait patiently until I was found or until the game was over. It felt that way watching everyone around me get chosen. Never even a bridesmaid, just a friend with a gift. A text came through my phone interrupting the tangent my mind had gone on. It was my friend Jasmine. Her birthday happened to be two days before mine and she was requesting my attendance at her get together. I replied yes but wasn't really in the mood to go out. It always felt like work. I shook the notion off and texted our mutual friend Felicia. I knew if I committed to meeting someone to go then I would actually go. Felicia and I decided we would meet at 6:30pm and head over together. Mentally, I began to prepare for this outing. Despite being the social butterfly in groups, I craved my solitude. It was also the reason I didn't mind being single. No one to answer to, come and go as I please and no one to give up the middle of the bed for. Chile that was my SPOT. I threw on my black faux leather suit and wool pea coat and off I went to meet Felicia. She arrived a few minutes after and we jumped on the train to our stop. The venue sign seemed to be the only prominent lighting on the street. We stopped in front of Chance 11, showed our ID and walked straight in to find Jasmine already having drinks. She seemed to be telling a story when she caught wind of us in her peripheral and quickly wrapped it up to greet us. "Hey Tavia, Hey Felicia! Thanks for coming! Go get a drink!" I slipped my coat off and walked over to the bar. Felicia and I decided to share a fishbowl then returned to the group. Jasmine rambled off names as we reappeared, and I began to drink our drink. Then I felt someone standing over me. "Hey H!" Jasmine squealed. "Where is Drew and Mel?" He responded, "I don't know but I made it" She gave him the same instruction givens to me upon my arrival. H tapped me on the shoulder. "Hi what's that?", pointing at my bowl. "It's a fish bowl." He looked puzzled and said, "What's in it?" I shrugged my shoulders and said, "Liquor" He smiled and went to the bar. Upon his return, I noticed that H was never too far from me. No matter where I went, he seemed to be close by. It started to annoy me. What the hell did he want? I asked Felicia, "Is this dude following me?!" She quickly dismissed the notion. "H is harmless. He's really laid back and can be shy. He's cool I promise." I took her advice and went on with the evening. We laughed, I flirted with other guys there. More people arrived and she decided to take pictures.

I got the bright idea to climb at the top of the white sofa to ensure I would be seen. It wasn't until it was time for me to get down that I realized how much I had to drink and had trouble getting down. H again never too far saw the concern in my face and quickly extended his hand and helped me down. Immediately, I thought "Gentleman". As though I was checking off an imaginary box. A couple group shots later and everyone began to gather their coats to go. I glanced at H again and this time I noticed how well his wool coat fit and how clean his shoes were. I liked his plaid shirt and slacks. I smiled then began to walk by the glass doors to exit. It had started to drizzle. Out the corner of my eye, I spot a drop top Benz pull up front. I'm not a car person but quickly chucked at how the car had to be rented. I mean what man would drive their expensive ass car with the top down in the rain. I could see him looking at me as he opened the door to get out. I looked to the side to happily see H right behind me. I grabbed his hand and said "Say we are together". H shrugged his shoulders ok. He opened the door and dude noticed our hands interlocked and detoured towards Jasmine.

Caught off guard, she quickly noticed how everyone was paired up but her and sighed that she had no choice but to entertain this dude.

"So what's your name?"

"Jazzy"

"My name is Joe; look how we go together.

Lemme get your number"

"Where's your phone?"

"It's broke, let me get a pencil."

Everyone walked away laughing.

Soon H and I reached the corner. My mind drifted to his hands. How big they were, how strong they were, yet they felt so soft. Then I heard his voice. "Do you want to keep holding hands or do you want to stop?" The question snapped me right out of my trance. I dropped his hand and apologized for holding it for so long. He smiled and told me it was cool but instantly I was embarrassed. Felicia and Jasmine caught up to us and we flagged a cab to go home. Jasmine and I lived blocks away from each other and H told Felicia he would crash on her couch until the morning because he lived far. She agreed and we hopped in. H sat in the front and we all got in the back. Felicia wasted no time telling me that H liked me. I looked up from my phone in shock. I mean this was the same man that basically asked me to let his hand go. I laughed at the notion and went back to looking at my Instagram page. We dropped Jasmine first. We all got out, hugged her goodbye and I told her I would see her in a few days for my birthday dinner.

My stop was next and H slid beside me in the back versus returning to the front seat with the driver. I could smell cologne suddenly and I liked it. Almost instantly, I remembered the last time I got some. I woke myself up just in time to let the driver know my coordinates. H got out to let me emerge from the car, taking my hand to ensure I didn't fall. I gave him a hug and before he let me go, he asked for my Instagram page handle. I gave it to him and followed back. I smirked and asked if he would approve of me. He smiled and said I already did. I refreshed my screen to show he did. "So H you coming to my dinner?", I slyly asked. "I wish I could but I have to work." I tried not to look disappointed. "Ok well maybe next time" I hugged Felicia and started walking towards my door. Then Felicia said, "You Know H, the only way Tavia would even notice you is if you like all the pictures on her page." We all laughed and I went inside. The next day I got up and got dressed to pick up some last-minute things for my birthday dinner. I was happy that it still wasn't freezing cold despite it being early November. My phone was in my pocket, and it started to vibrate uncontrollably. I rolled my eyes wondering who the hell was blowing up my phone. Of course, it took forever to get it in my hands to see that it was my Instagram notifications. It was H. Before I could unlock my phone, he had liked another picture, then another, then another until filled with only his notifications. I held my phone in awe. Was he really liking all of my pics? My answer would come in another ten minutes. My battery was half full but I didn't care. Then the last like but this one came with a note. "I'm not stalking you; I just wanted you to know I liked you." Then it came to me. I remembered Felicia's joke. This smile appeared that I had never felt before. I felt pursued. Usually, I pursued men. I dropped all the hints to let them know that they should ask me out. I had been so annoying to him. I basically called him a stalker and here I was smiling. I wished that he could be at my dinner. I didn't even ask for his number. Even though I knew at that moment, I liked him too. Later on that night, I looked through his pictures. There weren't many but in all of them he looked so happy. I loved his smile and his features. I wondered if I would ever see him again. More than anything I wondered why I couldn't get him off my mind. I promised myself that I wouldn't get consumed with this feeling. I wouldn't lose myself in him. I would stay focused and true to my heart. I mean it wasn't like he had done more than like some pictures.

The morning after, I woke up renewed. It wasn't only my birthday, but it was a new start.

A new understanding of who I was and what I wanted out of life. I felt whole. I felt excited. I was gonna get all dressed up and see my friends and my family. Soon the night came and I was surrounded by all the love in the world. My daughter was there and my sister. Friends I had seen in years. When the photographer arrived, I made sure to take pictures with everyone. The smile on my face never disappeared. Before I knew it the night ended, and I was off to Ohio to visit my favorite cousin. The month flew by and the holidays invaded in the air. I was in a wonderful space. I had good friends and great family. I no longer felt alone. I was truly happy not content with my life. New Year's Day was literally two days away and I was making plans to surprise Felicia with a club night with her favorite artist. We were on the phone talking about the logistics when she decided to scrap the plans to have a game night at her house. There would be food, and everyone would bring their own beverages. I was hoping for a good night. It didn't even occur to me to wonder about H until I walked through her door. I casually mentioned him, and Felicia let me know that he had gone to London to see his family and wasn't sure if he would be by. I shrugged off the notion but every time the door opened my heart skipped a beat. I was anxious. Her friends started to show up and I got comfortable on the couch besides her roommate. We made small talk, played a couple games and time ticked on.

Then there was a knock at the door. I look up to find everyone greeting H. There he was wearing his wool coat and plaid shirt and blue slacks. He made sure to speak to everyone as he walked through the room. Then our eyes met. He bent down and hugged me. Everything after was a blur. Time passed and people began to leave. Until soon it was just me, H, Felicia and her roommate. I got hungry and got up to cook some food I brought over. He jumped up and offered to help. I walked to the kitchen and he asked what I needed him to do. He grabbed the bowl and opened the packaging for the fish, and I grabbed the seasoning.

"So how was your Christmas?" he asked.

"It was good. I heard you went to London."

"Yeah, I went with my mom to see my aunt and cousins. I was supposed to stay two weeks but decided to only stay a week."

"Oh, never been to London. How long is the flight?"

"Umm 6 hours."

"So I have a question. You liked all my pictures, said you liked me then never asked for my number? What's up with that?"

"I thought we would bump into each other sooner. Didn't think I should ask you that online."

thoughts hmm manners

"So I have a question. Why are you single?" he said.

"I'm single because I haven't found what I needed." His eyebrow raised.

"What do you need?"

"Someone that can handle my moods, make me laugh, be a good friend to my daughter, give me space when I need it and fuck me whenever want." I replied.

"I could do that." He said so matter of fact.

"Oh really." I replied.

"Why are you single?"

"I guess I haven't found what I needed."

Of course I asked. "What do you need?"

"Someone who likes to eat. Likes to spend time with me. Won't lie to me or pretend. Someone who is honest and caring. Who wants to fuck me whenever I want." Then he laughed.

thoughts smart ass

"Do you think you can give me that?" I asked, staring in his eyes.

"If you let me" he replied with a smile.

I felt my loins warm. I felt something that I couldn't remember ever feeling. I felt safe. We retired back to the couch. Sharing the food we made together and before I knew it the TV was counting down to the next year. I looked in his eyes and said Happy New Year and before he could complete the sentiment he kissed me. I felt like I had been waiting for that kiss my whole life. The kiss lingered on and I could feel the bulge in his slacks. He backed up a bit once he realized I did. I asked him quietly, "Now what?" He replied, "I guess we're not single anymore." I took out my iPad and told him I wanted to take a picture to remember this night. I told him not to look in the camera in case we didn't work out. I snapped it and sent it to my phone. That was the beginning of us. That was January 1, 2014. On February 13, 2015, I gave birth to our son. On April 26, 2015, H asked me to be his wife. On July 7, 2017, we got married in the middle of Prospect Park and together we remain almost 7 years later. This is the most honest, loving and hardest relationship I have ever been in but no matter what happens there is love. No matter how often we disagree, no matter how often we annoy each other, no matter how moody I become, he is always there. The night before our wedding I found that note that I wrote in my notebook. The note I woke up out of my sleep to write. The one that I poured my heart into writing and I laughed. From my mouth to God's ears. The bible says "He who finds a wife finds a good thing, and obtains favor from the Lord." Now I don't sit in church every Sunday but my faith in God is unwavering. It wasn't until that moment that I realized that it was not my job to find H. He had to find me. So, every day I thank him for doing just that, finding me.

Note to Self

More to Say..

Chapter Six

I Was Lost But Now I'm Found

I spent so much time wanting to be the Boss. Operating off the sentiment that a closed mouth don't get fed. Fighting to be seen by men that looked good on paper. Changing who I was once I had them, then losing them to other women that re-enacted the fire I once possessed. I was guarded. I was scorned. I was jaded and I was unsure of who I was and what I wanted yet I blamed the other person for not giving me their all. I made every man around me feel like I didn't need them, ultimately confusing them when good sex made me believe I did. I changed the rules and kept everyone at bay to ensure I wasn't hurt. But hurt people, hurt people.

Probably the realist statement I ever read. You can't place expectations on anyone else. You shouldn't hold people accountable for not sacrificing themselves when you wouldn't do it either. But none of that will become evident to you until you realize that your pussy ain't shit. Having a good pussy and giving good head won't make someone not lie to you. It won't make someone not cheat on you or hurt you or mentally abusive you. It won't keep them home at night. It won't make them give you their all. It is merely a bonus. Anyone of substance needs more and craves more from you. They need to feel a connection. They need to feel like you are what they have been looking for. You need to know what you're looking for. You gotta know what truly makes your heart flutter and then be realistic. No one is perfect and it won't be easy. But you gotta make that list. You gotta know your deal breakers. Then you gotta be willing to settle for nothing less. If not, you will never have true love. You will never know what it feels like to know that someone other than you, loves you unconditionally. Bad breath, messy hair, flaws and all.

The key to any good relationship is love of thyself first. You can't be the man in the relationship and want a man. You can be strong without making others feel weak. You can be aggressive without being overpowering. You can't control everything. Shoot you don't control much as soon as you think you have control, life happens. Sometimes it might even feel like it's too much to bear. But those are times you remember who you are. You remember your faith. You remember that everything good in life starts with loving yourself. You have nothing to give anyone else until you give to yourself first. Why do you think they ask you to put the mask on yourself then whoever you're with? If the airlines think you should come first, why don't you.

It's not selfish to love yourself. It's not selfish to feel like you matter or to think highly of yourself. Now I'm not saying to be condescending or to be egotistical. Everything needs to be in balance. What I am saying is that no one should be able to affect how you feel about you. It's called self-esteem for a reason. So, if no one tells you this today, I love you. You are doing a good job. You can always do better. You need to figure your shit out. You need to dress like someone cares about you and if that is nobody it's me. I'm the friend you wish you had, the one you haven't met that knows how awesome you are. So, you're welcome. You made it. You lasted. You persevered. Now you gotta do the work. Yes, the work. The thing that everyone keeps talking about. The effort you make to unpack your luggage and move on with an open heart and mind. The moment when you feel so free you start to sound psychological. Like you have a degree in shit because you have been somewhere and go through some things. It's a marathon not a race. Some of us get it sooner than others. I didn't get it until I was 34 years old. I couldn't grasp it because I was lost. I was searching for something that I had to find within myself. It sounds so simple but it's not. That is why I wrote this. So maybe it can open a space in your mind to let you know that you are not alone. That someone has been there. Not exactly there but close enough to help you get to the next phase in your life. Another person should never complete you, they should enhance you. They should motivate you. Remind you that you're the shit. All of you. From the top of your head to the bottom of your feet. Everything about you is amazing and no matter what you deserve love. You deserve respect and they deserve to receive it back. If you're not ready to love anyone, that is ok. Loving yourself is the only thing you need to get on the ball with. You are stuck with you forever. Until God calls you home this is your life. So, get on it. Get to it and I will be here to tell you, I knew you could do it. I knew you could win. You are in the fight of your life and failing isn't an option. Until next time, be well and give yourself some credit! Your eyes are open and you have successfully finished this manual. So, what are you gonna do?

Last Last:

1. **Self-Awareness Exercise**
   - What are three moments in your life when you felt truly connected to yourself?
   - Are there any behaviors or patterns you've held onto that no longer serve you? Write about them and how you might begin to release them.

2. **Relationship Inventory**
   - Think about past relationships. What qualities were you seeking, and were those qualities fulfilled?
   - What did you learn about yourself from those relationships?

3. **Self-Love Check-In**
   - List three things you genuinely love about yourself.
   - Are there any areas of your life where you feel like you've been putting others' needs above your own? How can you create balance?

Activities:

1. **The Deal Breaker List**
   - Write down your non-negotiables in relationships (romantic, platonic, or professional).
   - Beside each deal breaker, write a positive value or action that aligns with what you truly want.

2. **Daily Affirmation Journal**

- For one week, write down one affirmation each day that reinforces your self-worth and self-love. Examples:
    - "I am deserving of love and respect."
    - "My happiness begins with me."

3. **Unpacking the Luggage**
    - Write a letter to your past self acknowledging the pain, lessons, and growth you've experienced. Once finished, decide if you want to keep it as a reminder or symbolically release it (e.g., by shredding it or storing it away).

Key Takeaway Questions:

- What does "loving yourself first" mean to you?
- How will you remind yourself daily that your value is inherent and doesn't depend on external validation?
- What is one small, actionable step you can take today to prioritize self-love and growth?

Note to Self

More to Say..

Dedication

This manual is dedicated to my aunt who I aspire to be like in every way that matters, my uncle who loves me no matter what, my daughter who loved me before I understood what love was, my son who would rather be no place else but with me, my husband who found me after I found myself, my Twin whose friendship means more than she knows and last to Charles Jr. and Georgiana who I carry with me always.

Forever Yours, Tav

www.ingramcontent.com/pod-product-compliance
Lightning Source LLC
Chambersburg PA
CBHW052034030426
42337CB00027B/4999